Resuscitation
ROB MACDONALD Party

Resuscitation

ROB MACDONALD

Party

Racing
Form
Press

Boston Portland

Resuscitation Party
©2015 Rob MacDonald   All rights reserved

ISBN: 978-0-9895611-6-7

Printed in the USA   First Edition, 2015

Set in Racing Form Text, designed by Thomas Jockin

Cover by Shira Richman

Racing Form Press titles are available through Small Press
Distribution and their website.

www.racingformpress.com

TABLE OF CONTENTS

I

1

BITTERSWEET

every time we drove past the Domino Sugar factory
Steve would point and ask how sweet would it be to
work there   some questions are meant to be hung
like photographs of phone booths in bathrooms
we were much too young to know how far life's
memorable moments might spread out   next time
you order coffee watch more carefully as you pour
the sugar in   most grains disappear in an instant
others fade after a little stir   you may feel sad but
you have to remember that you're about to drink
them and turn them into your new eyes

LIFEBOAT

I get scared when I think
big ships,

ocean liners
with multiple pools.

Which deck is safe
in case of hail,

in case of volcano?
39 straight days of rain

do not a refund make.
To be untethered,

to be without walls—
ideas can't bounce

off salt air alone.
An absence of ideas

can't turn a propeller.
And these people,

eating their
baked ziti and waiting

for cheesecake—
I get scared.

HOW TO SURVIVE CHILDHOOD

A heart like a wiffleball.

An old boat hull
in which daisies grow.

When you're alone
with a jackknife

and the swamp
is all cattail.

A few firecrackers
in isolation

never hurt anyone.

HOW YOU STARTED WRITING

First, you discovered nothing
and wanted to show it off
to your friends.

Pointing at nothing
proved problematic, though,
so you circled it.

See? you said, so proud.
With no shortage of absence,
you found plenty

of nothingness to circle,
your loops getting lazy
or crazed, angular,

incomplete. And soon
the loops were something,
the beautiful between.

GRACE OUT

During recess at St. Catherine's Elementary,
Thomas spots a coral snake,
and because he is good, he picks it up
and carries it away from his classmates,
his teachers, away from you,
and keeps walking
because you should never know
what it feels like
to be the conduit—
two holes in the palm of your hand:
sin in, grace out.

CONCENTRATE

The father from Montreal
ordered breakfast on behalf
of his family. *Two fresh eggs,*
he asked for, and we didn't know

what to do. It was the quickest
summer ever—just a few days
to chase beautiful girls
across the beach—so it wasn't

sex. We blamed cultural
differences for the lack of tips,
so it wasn't money. We rescued
sisters from their grandparents'

off-white ranch late at night
before realizing we had nothing
to offer them except the sound
of waves breaking against

a concrete wall. We broke up
the band. We had to wear aprons
every morning, so it wasn't pride.
We spent our Sundays religiously

filling champagne flutes with
orange juice from concentrate,
but no one could ever illuminate
what the father wanted.

FETAL POSITION

Jon tells me
about a girl
who wants

to put her hair
inside his
belly button.

It's a thing,
he says.
Alabaster,

a big
horny afro.
The roar,

the wrench
that every
belly button

encloses.
She wants
to fill him

with hair
and cross
sex deserts.

I say Jon,
this girl has
so many

bad ideas,
but he says
it's okay to

keep being
born again
and again.

DEAD MAN'S FLOAT

At the pool party,
we're all washed out.

I can barely see
my eyesore shorts,

but we exist,
for better or worse.

We use the roof
of the brown van

as a chance to survey
our slippery lives

before cannonballing
into one another's skulls.

Someone goes blind.
Someone spills

rum and Coke
all over the whole afternoon.

The white bikinis
are immaculate,

but we can't figure out
what it is

we're supposed to say,
how we're supposed to

survive this
terrible togetherness.

CEDE

On our first date,
both of us
gazed down upon
deforestation
through a hole
in a cloud,

clasped hands
and lungless
timber spangles,
a little secret
massacre
just for us.

You looked
into my mouth,
wondering
what I'd cede,
and I said
nothing.

OVERCOMING THE URGE TO SEE THE WORLD

I was told
to spend a night
inside a department store—
a vision quest of sorts.

In my sleep,
I saw shadows
of chintzy little bicycles,
asymmetric spokes.

I awoke
with assurance
that staying in one place
is the new motion.

The world
isn't waiting
for me to invent some sort
of enormous wings.

You aren't
waiting for me
to carry you away from this
shabby fluorescence.

REGRESSION WITH APPLE IIC

In 1986, I got beat up
and thrown in a jacuzzi
full of Diet Pepsi.

Henry printed me
a birthday banner
with the sprockets

torn off so cleanly,
and then everything
was okay again. Nothing

gave me cavities,
not even the girl
at the video store.

No naked nightmares
or shuddering,
but hope did

hold me down
while misery kicked.
I kept getting throttled,

and Henry kept
finding new
Print Shop combos

that brought me
back to something
he called life.

JUVENILIA

Tonight, I'm intent on raiding the hen house.

The moon makes me stupid, and once I've lost my head,
it's chicken or nothing.

Studying the stars for hints about my pre-existence
would be a better habit,
but I want to paint my name in eggs on the broad side
of that fucking barn.

I want them to name a comet in my honor, and then
I want the comet to drape me in flames.

Take that, hen house.

Take that, barn.

WHAT WE SAVED

It was the winter of black
construction paper—

the kind you poke through
with plastic pegs

to show your family
you're going supernova.

We watched tracer fire
unzip the sky. We had the dust

of Pandora's terracotta jar
sprinkled over our dreaming eyes.

It was easy to be angry.
It was easy to buy CDs

full of guitars' screaming.
The new era was enamored

with flying toasters.
In truth, the room was empty,

and you had trouble deciding
whether to think or simply

press a series of buttons.
It was possible you'd create

something important.
It was possible you'd rescue

a princess who never existed.
Everything seemed to be circling

a celestial TV, all of us unsure
how many light years ago

its cathodes had died.
We didn't know our own

neighborhood's name,
but we did find some comfort

in Salvation Army flannel,
a chance to live in the skin

of something simple.
Remember how much easier it got

to hear all the crying?
We can abandon one another,

guilt-free, as soon as
our dreams leave for college.

We can accept our affliction—
it's the electric hum

we're so accustomed to
we case pillows in it.

Do you remember
the starry nights of the '90s,

how our screens resisted sleep?
We used to distinguish

nightmare from memory
by color palette, but now

both are binary while
nothing is black and white.

MID-CENTURY / MODERN

Thinking back to the house
I grew up in—

the cheap carpet, the freezer
full of frozen pizza,

the Eames leather lounge
and ottoman—

I think I must have had two
sets of parents:

those who saw candlepin bowling
strikes in slow-mo

and those who skittered off
when the kitchen lights came on.

SHE WALKS TO THE SEA

I know what   bossa nova is
thanks to the people   at Casio
who made   my first calculator.
There's a rhythm   to arithmetic
and a proper way   to play guitar.
Absence   makes all the difference.
The college kids   are starting
to wear   white shoes again;
they must be   mermaids.

THE PROBLEM WITH FLORIDA

The problem with Florida
is that the streets are teal
and the yellow lines are
teal, so no one can tell
where one dude ends
and another begins.
Plus, the large bugs
constantly revving
their legs—I can't
even hear what
your radio is
gnashing.

PURITAN ROOTS

I've been suffering
from the Y2K bug
since the late '90s,
when suffering was
falling out of fashion
and all of the worst
walls had already
fallen. The world is
supposedly getting
smaller each year,
which explains all
of the low ceilings
in the downtown lofts.
This, in turn, explains
the rise in concussions,
which explains why
the bar isn't set
so high at the finest
academic institutions.
If our undergrads
are underprepared
and overindulgent,
that explains why
the stock futures are
falling faster each year,
like the prices of
memory sticks, which
it doesn't, unless you
study all night, unless
you connect events
to sensory cues
like the dumplings
that accompany
my fuzzy memory
of our first date,

Boston, so salty,
or all the blood
in the steaks of our
second date—who can
say how long ago we
met?—which makes me
wonder how long
we've been suffering.

BREAKDOWN

Sometimes, when I'm driving
late at night toward nothing
in particular, I think of
Eisenhower, who was treated
like a real hero after
he had his highways built.
He didn't live long enough
to see his granddaughters'
disfigured pickups,
and some would say
that's for the best, but
sometimes, when I'm driving,
I think, *Am I doing any good,*
teaching my America
to think cynically, to plot
the new world from the top
of an old, rickety bridge?
We might all be insulating
the nursery walls with
asbestos, painting the most
peaceful scenes on the crib
in lead. I won't even wear
a seatbelt; let me be
thrown free, far from this
flaming wreck of a debt.

GRIND

You come to me
Wednesday afternoon

bearing Doritos
in a swarm of bees.

You come to me
with dead batteries

and a flyer
on privatized water.

You have a bag of laundry
slung over your shoulder,

and I can smell
the dirty sheets.

It's not easy—
we're dying to be dancing

like go-go girls
in a San Diego bar

that never existed,
but you come to me,

Reality, with so many
unpaid bills in your fist.

INFLATIONS

At the private school
in the hills,

I ask the teacher
what they mean

by "gifted."
She explains

some students
are virtuosos,

"really gifted" kids
running hedge funds

and scribbling
little symphonies.

Others, she says,
are "regular gifted."

I leave the school
feeling like

a real star,
like a stripe.

BACONATOR

When I was sixteen, I couldn't
eat a Baconator because
it didn't exist. At thirty-six,
I know it will fill me with evil,
and I want so much
to live a life of meaning,
leaving tiny explosions of yes
in my sensible sedan's wake,
helping kids see numbers' grace
in flocks of Canada geese
and vice versa, swallowing
curses as often as possible
despite the distracting insistence
of this world's extras
on texting through the reunion tour,
curling increasingly heavy metals
in hopes of maintaining
some culturally acceptable semblance
of masculinity, burning
only the slips of paper on which
what's done is done, moving on,
trusting in the potential
for microscopic daily miracles
to swell, maybe not
a democracy, but a chorus,
like the crickets this August,
listening to all of you
who might, at any moment,
misspeak and solve the riddle
of infinity—I want a Baconator,
and I do not want it.
At eighty, I'll simply be afraid.

FEED

Zoz tells me that people eat guinea pig in Peru,
and I don't say much because I've got a mouth-
ful of peanut butter and jelly. Some of our students
are allergic and would need to be stabbed
in the thigh with epinephrine to survive my lunch.
I eat and listen and think about Peru. It's easy.
The tough part is the flight back, the way the wings
get slick with rain, the way the whole city seems
innocuous from above, the way the cranberry juice
keeps nearly spilling during our endless descent.

JUPITER

I'm climbing the stairs of the motel in Florida and see some
twenty-somethings sitting outside their rooms in plastic chairs,
chain-smoking, waiting for Domino's to be delivered. They
nod as I pass, and I know what's wrong with America. I'm
the problem, and we teach just enough history to bring the
unavoidable future into focus. What I know is that I don't want
to smell their smoke from inside my room as I watch CNN;
explosions of awareness are killing innocent people all over the
planet.

HOW WE SPENT

Some of my students
fold a shirt
at Banana Republic
all summer.

Some of them teach
quiet kids
how to roar
at the world.

Some simply wait
for rain, for streetlights,
for what passes
for silence in the city.

The other students
spend every fall
using *summer*
as a verb.

UNFOLDING

Online, I learned
to find little cranes
and unfold them
into perfect sheets
of uncreased paper.
I learned to stack
the sheets into
rainbows, wrap
each spectrum
in cellophane,
send each stack
back to Japan
in an envelope
the color of air.
I find peace
in the undoing.
In the undoing,
I find peace.

THE COLONEL'S ORIGINAL RECIPE

I don't really know what makes good things good, but if the world had a few minutes left, I'd call you and ask you to meet me at the beach. Maybe I'd wear my white suit and some well-polished shoes. If you want to kiss in the sand, we'll kiss in the sand and stare at a cosmos full of madness. It's almost almost over, for whatever that's worth, so try to enjoy the way the waves insist on mumbling. I don't really know what you mean to me, but I know that we're here for a reason, and we're hungry for something, and if you say finger-lickin' good, I say let's die dumb.

PHASE SHIFT, MASSACHUSETTS

When I'm most awake
and the night road
is most open,
I just keep driving
past the Stop & Shop.

There's a station
between the stations
that plays
a comforting pulse,
and I'm ready.

DONUTS

In this town,
we do donuts

all night
while it snows

because circles
are the only

immortality
this town knows.

SLOW ROTATION

A steamroller seat
has no bars
to bookend your ass,
no seatbelt
to cinch you in.
Its armrestlessness
prevents no
sitters from falling
and getting pressed.
Do not let your
daughters ride
legs akimbo
atop this beast.
Let the frost heaves
heave. One minute
you're a real person,
the next a pancake.
That's the way
this world works;
like a Saturday
morning cartoon
with more wailing.
All the friends
I've forgotten
and the ones
who've forgotten
me—I try to
peel them from
the pavement,
but they're gone.

2

FLIGHTLESS

The flight was overbooked, so they gave us free passes to the zoo.
We dragged our luggage down the path, past the gorillas and
the giraffes. The place smelled nothing like a plane. We were all
thinking of home, how simple it was to adjust the thermostat, to
get a glass of milk from the fridge. Without speaking, we had all
agreed that we wanted no part of the skies ever again. It made
sense at the time—walking around and around the zoo until it
turned into our lives.

EXPAT / SEXPOT

Southbound, Erica says
she wishes eucalyptus didn't
look so much like apocalypse.

Erica never looks
her future directly
in the eyes.

It hits a hundred,
dizzy, and she's like
a walking skinny dip.

At a rest area, Erica tells you
it's rude to stare
at kids playing Yiri.

When the country runs out,
she says it's time to invest
in an inner tube.

She peels off her past
and asks you to kiss
the corner of the map.

JUST ENOUGH

In one version of the world, there is just enough of everything. You're scrambling to find candles for your niece's birthday cake, and there in the drawer, waiting—exactly eight. The bookstore where you're hosting a reading has twenty-five folding chairs, and that's the precise number of bums that show up. It's a magic that no one takes for granted. In fact, we're all so thrilled with this subsistence existence that we decide to throw a worldwide party one night, everyone invited. Clean up is easy—not a drop of wine, not a crumb remains. The next day, as we're picking grapes and baking, staring smitten into space, it will be too soon to see we've ruined it—we've all fallen in love with the same girl.

HALF-AWAKENING

I order carrot cake because
I'm in the mood for something
that should be orange but isn't,

like full-blown happiness.

After dessert, I take a walk.
I wave a plane down
from the everyday night

and wake all of the passengers up.

Half-awakening. Nowhere near us,
an unnamed planet glows orange,
rubbing it in, letting it sting.

JONAH PONDERS THE PROS AND CONS

I awoke only to find a realtor
showing the whale's stomach

to a young couple. They wore
blindfolds, blissfully oblivious

to the realtor's spiel:
A bit musty, but nothing

a dehumidifier couldn't fix.
Something about a sump pump

and an occasional ocean view.
I tried to mind my own business.

The couple drifted, held hands,
kissed as they waded through krill.

ROOFTOP APOCALYPSE PARTY

The End is on call tonight,
so it might be time
to type up some new lungs.

Local cops take notice—
I am reinventing reinvention.
I'm on to the next thing

like a fruit fly. Let's not
pretend we can swim
in flimsy t-shirts forever.

Okay, panic. A new prophet is
bombing the block with
old promises. And you—

your blue raspberry lips,
your authentic doe-eyed
throttle. Resuscitate me.

TEST

A man walked into my classroom during a test and said he'd been shot. Blood bubbled from a hole in his shoulder. My students took copious notes. One of them asked, "Was the shooter a stranger?" "No," the man answered. Another asked, "Is it more of a throbbing pain or a constant ache?" "Yes," he said. The questions continued for quite some time: "Will you live each day with a greater sense of urgency and purpose?" "Yes." "Could you see the bullet approaching in slo-mo?" "No." "Has this incident eradicated what little faith you had in humanity?" "Yes." All of my students were able to predict his last words, so they earned extra credit. I drew smiley faces atop all of their tests.

TEN STEPS

In this version,
you get ten steps,
then you're dead.

Where you're born
is so important—

mothers in labor
on the banks
of the Ganges,

in the bleachers
at Wrigley.

You stood still
for the first
thirty years,

desperate to determine
the ideal direction,

hoping to step
slowly enough
to fully absorb

the glory
of motion.

Meanwhile, all
the lovers running
toward one another,

young arms
outstretched.

ORIGIN STORY, PERPETUAL UNDERDOG

Your father was a left-fielder
with a knack for snow-cone catches,

putting out grease fires in Chinese kitchens,

building custom rocking chairs
from windblown oaks,

manning the phones at a call center
on a riverboat,

investing in marbles and losing it all.

Mom read the rough drafts
and chiseled saints into baby teeth.

WHATEVER THE OPPOSITE OF HYPOCHONDRIA IS

Things got so fucked
that our summer vacation
consisted of a series of trips
to CVS.

I asked if I could put
a plastic bag over my head.
My little brother made castles
out of aspirin.

By the end of August,
our faces were plastered
on the lukewarm half gallons
of 2% milk.

You think this is me
lying, but this poem is
a placebo. These lines are
eye medicine.

BODY COMMODIFICATION

At the yard sale, I saw that they were selling all my stuff. It was
flattering to see so many people grabbing at my past, traffic
blocked in both directions, strangers stopping and parking
and leaving doors ajar. I was actually proud until I noticed
how much haggling was going on: a quarter for my Mardi Gras
beads, two bucks for my hunting permit, fifty cents for my whole
hip-hop collection. *This is a joke,* I think I thought. All night, I
sat in someone else's yard, watching the slow erosion of my own
existence. When a single mom bought my body, I objected, but
my eyes, by that time, were cloudy marbles.

REDUCED SENTENCE or SNAGGLEPUSS PONDERS HIS OWN MORTALITY

This motel must belong to Betsy.
It must be Murgatroyd's, even.
There's no bible in my nightstand—
what a chintzy little outfit!
But look at all the angels
in the pool tonight—seraphim
and cherubim treading water
under the moon, already.
What wickedness this way comes,
pray tell? What's going on,
that is? I should've shelled out
the extra two bits for more
accommodating accommodations.
No mints under the pillow.
No pillow, even. They lock the gate
at I AM. Exit, no exit. I should've
saved up for that South Seas cruise.
Those sirens are my cues—
one great escape coming up.
One fraidy cat checking out.

OCCASION

I was shopping for wrapping paper at the drug store when a
woman stopped beside me. "What's the occasion?" she asked.
"No occasion," I said. "No occasion? Are you some kind of pervert?
Murderer? Terrorist?" She grabbed a pink gift bag and started
filling it with balloons, birthday candles, wedding invitations and
ribbons. "Here you go, you filthy bastard!" she screamed. "Have
a party! Everyone's invited! Who wants to get stabbed? Who
wants to get left for dead on the side of the highway?" I tried
to calm her down, but nothing was working. In the end, I had
to put on a clown wig and make a run for it. That night, when I
told my wife, she said that I should have strangled the life from
the woman and put her in the trunk of my car and brought her
body home and buried it beside the willow tree with all the rest.
I didn't know what to say. My wife, after all, does have a degree
from a well-respected university, and I can barely tie my own
shoes. When I wrap a present, it looks like it's been wrapped by
a child.

WHEN TO SHUT YOUR MOUTH

My teeth are a levee—
otherwise, who knows?
My sister-in-law

says she's looking forward
to being outwardly insane,
filling her winter coat

with Honey Nut Cheerios.
Yeah.
And the ideal ending…

but I don't open my mouth,
so it sounds like *idle*
or *idol.* Don't tell them

how deeply you believe
in Greg Brady's tiki.
Dreams are like jokes

are like syndicated shows—
they wither
under close inspection.

LOS LOBOS

Somehow, I ended up in Los Lobos, and my suit didn't fit. Cesar told me not to be a pussy. He said, "Life is an unsolved murder, my friend," except he didn't say "my friend." When we took the stage, I was careful not to smile. It was my funeral, maybe. I had a colony of bats in my eyes, and they were ready for independence.

COACH

I got a job as a gym teacher at a school in the suburbs. They
called me "Coach" even though I didn't do any coaching. Each
day, I told the children to run in circles. Each day, the circles got
bigger; this helped them develop endurance. At the end of every
class, I explained to them that endurance was the key to a happy
life, or at worst, a long unhappy one. The kids, of course, as they
ran in circles, always eyed the red playground balls. Rumors
spread about a parachute in the storage closet. One afternoon,
a boy who was a particularly slow runner knocked on my door.
When I told him to come in, I could see that he had been crying;
it must have been a lot of crying, because he was soaking wet all
the way from his eyes down to his toes. He was making a mess
of my office, leaving little puddles on the carpet. "What's the
problem?" I asked. "Coach," he said, "I think my heart is broken.
Whenever I run, it hurts." "How long has this been happening," I
asked. "All year," he said. "And Coach, it's getting worse. Now
it hurts even when I walk." It was a serious moment, but I was a
good teacher. I told him it would all be fine, and the next day, I
gave him a flash drive full of Nirvana songs. I even took him to
the Salvation Army and helped him pick out a mustard-colored
cardigan. Before long, he was getting picked on and spending
recess in the art room. Some of the teachers started to worry
about him, so, during one of our faculty meetings, I had to go up
to the front of the room and explain endurance. The response
was overwhelming; they made me the new guidance counselor
right away. Now, they call my replacement "Coach." He's a
horse's ass; our kids seem to be walking slower than ever.

IN SEARCH OF OUR STUPID INNER SELVES

We built a kayak out of bone
and crescented so far south
we lost all ability to reason.

I forgot how to make a cursive *k,*
and you couldn't multiply
to save your life.

Drinking from the red river
was the new cannibalism,
but our shame was gone, too.

The bone, so efficient,
cut through the algae
like an abandoned idea,

like a choir of like-minded
residents of a simple town,
full of faith, far from home,

white light erupting from
their simultaneous throats
even before we reach the shore.

RECEIVER

The night before the phones were scheduled to be cut off for good, I picked up my landline and listened. Beneath the dial tone, a conversation emerged. He wanted her to join him in California, but she wanted to stay in New York, near her family. I hung up. Picked up again. This time, he wanted her to wear brighter colors, and she wanted him to have a lower center of gravity. All night, they argued, paraphrasing the various voices that rented their heads. Looking closely at the old phone gave me some ideas about the ratio between the number of holes it takes to talk and the number it takes to listen.

FIVE SONS

you have five sons & name them   one two three four five
it's tough to overcome emotions   but you try to adore them

equally   charting forehead kisses to ensure consistency
halfway through the study   they learn to subtract   two

of them are fighting with sticks   & you yell negative one
the project calls for identical ties   your graduate assistant

asks you why   you didn't just name them subject   everyone
expects five to be arrested   but he plays viola   whenever one

turns seventeen   you put him through extensive tests
an obstacle course & scan his brain   while he paints   three

seems to be   left-handed & pretty   quiet   you publish
their IQ scores   in a journal of mathematics   the five sons

scatter   oslo tunis tempe fresno fargo   a librarian wants to
date you   marry you hyphenate you   you spend so much

time in the study   proving nothing   at the end of every day
five postcards on a desk   five notes in your wine

DISARMED

There was a knock at the door, and when I answered it, the chief of police was there. "Sir," he said, removing his hat, "I'm sorry to say that there's a serial killer loose in the neighborhood, so be on the lookout." "For what?" I said. "Well, this particular killer seems to have a thing for garden tools. The first one was done with a trowel, then came the rake, then a hanging by hose—you get the idea," the chief said. It sounded sort of romantic, but I stifled a smile. "Thanks so much for warning me," I said. "So, if I see him, what should I do?" The chief was silent, and he shuffled his big feet for a moment. Leaves began to fall from the trees. "I suppose you should scream," he said. "Oh," I said. "That makes sense. I could scream *fire!* to try to scare him away." "No, that might create a panic, sir. I'd prefer that you scream *hoser!* or *rakist!* These days, we can never be too specific," the chief said. "I see," I said. "And if he's coming at me with a hoe?" The chief looked puzzled. "I've never heard of murder by hoe, but you may be on to something," he said, and then he deputized me, but all I got was a midnight blue windbreaker. We've been working the case for weeks now, and I find that I'm starting to think like a killer, confusing death and growth all the time. I can't pass a cornfield without wondering who's running from me, without wanting to show them how empty my pockets are—I'm utterly disarmed.

DH

Batter up
is what they say

when Cake Tartare
comes to the plate.

Cake leads the league
in sacrifice flies.

Cake is dating
an exotic dancer.

These days,
Cake can only DH;

he's icing his elbow
after every game,

can't catch up
with the high heat,

and his wheels aren't
what they used to be.

Cake wants to be
frosted, chocolate,

dessert at some
nursing home,

the strange taste
of the last day

of some stranger's
normal life.

FORMAL INTRODUCTION

I'm total broke,
fishing pro,
kissing missing teeth.

I'm bowling alone,
smoking birch
in fucking first place.

Who came to work
with bird shit on
and nothing underneath?

The beast of mean
is me, and I have
cummerbund for thee.

CAPTIVATED

The key to the TV show about cloning
is simultaneous consciousness,

controlling two bodies at once—
not a familiar other,

but a true second self.
You're you, and you're shaking

your hand, and you're feeling
both sets of knuckles.

It's like an angular octopus.
Of course, our fascination

with the clean slate leads to
hybrid homicide/suicide.

It's murder/makeover, and
it's killing the primetime ratings.

All the crossover potential
(crossbows, Bowflex, low T treatment...),

and then the pendulum swings
to baby shows, then embryos,

a deep red screen and nothing
but the sound of a tiny heart beating.

LOVE POEM

I kill eels
and huck them
from the roof.
They've got
a hundred floors
to fall, which is
just enough time
to become
butterflies.
On the hood
of a cab.
On your hand,
little wings
inhaling.

BOLINUS BRANDARIS

Don't eat the grapes—
they're someone else's

bruises. If nothing
heals, nothing knows
the loop of life.

A horse, too thin,
walks the beach

alone, drinks
from tide pools
until a swarm

of hornets take pity—
a million of them

lift the horse,
spine sagging,
over the dunes

and into
the vineyard.

HOW WE DROWNED

When the earthquake hit,
I was peeling an apple,

but it wasn't an earthquake,
and it wasn't an apple—

we were in Atlantis again,
waiting for the sea floor

to stop trembling, and you
were removing a mask

to prove that you were not
just another character.

We were in the Atlantis
that spit lava ribbons

and bubbled white smoke
to the surface, and you

were removing a mask
to reveal a heartbreaking

lifespan. We don't last long,
and we screw around

with words, pretending
we're not real—not *real* real.

I was peeling an apple,
and it was spelling something,

but I was too worried
about my gushing heart

to see the letters. Or dog paddle
from death. Or take it all in.

ACKNOWLEDGMENTS

Many thanks to the editors of the following journals where some of these poems first appeared:

The Bakery, B O D Y, Death Hums, elsewhere, esque, The Fiddleback, Gulf Coast, Harpur Palate, Horse Less Review, I Thought I Was New Here, ILK, inter/rupture, Jellyfish, Jellyroll, The Journal, jubilat, Leveler, Map Literary, NAP, Phantom Limb, SCUD, Sink Review, So and So, Tuesday: An Art Project and *Whiskey Island.*

BIOGRAPHY

Rob MacDonald is the author of the chapbook *Situation Normal* (Rye House Press, 2015). His poems have appeared in *Birdfeast, H_NGM_N, Washington Square, Octopus,* and other journals. He lives in Boston and is the editor of *Sixth Finch.*